ALEXANDER STARK

A SIREN'S WAIL

– FEMINISM EXPOSED –

Table of Content

Instruction Manual

Within this book, literary sources are marked with a name and year in parentheses, e.g. (Andersen, 2013). Details can be found in the bibliography at the end of this book, it is alphabetically sorted by name. Wherever applicable, the bibliography entries also show an internet address to access the source online.

Four of these sources are written in German. If you feel the need to review those sources in depth, please consider learning this wonderful language; there is no other that stands for love and tolerance as much as German. If you're in a hurry, though, you might just utilize one of the machine translation services available on the internet.

Well, that should cover the basics. Let's go!

Foreword

"I hate feminism. It is poison."
(Margaret Thatcher)

In this book, we will set out to explore the hostile and dangerous waters of feminism. There's a lot of fog, and the surface seems like a mirror, but closely underneath sharp riffs and horrific creatures lurk. Sirens sing their song, but don't despond! Let this book be your wax, tear off its pages and stick them into your ears, and you will laugh and prevail.

You will gain knowledge that you wish you never acquired. Life won't be the same. We will shed light into the darkest corners and examine the evil creatures lurking there. Chances are, you already heard them hissing, you already smelled their foul stench, you already felt them creeping closer every day, every hour, every minute.

Yes. *Them*. Feminists.

Not the harmless idealists that actually have no real idea about feminism, who only know Gloria Steinem for her Seventies disco hit "I Will Survive" and simply mistake feminism for egalitarianism. Can we blame them?

No. They're cute. Sometimes.

This seems to be a good time to bring up the necessary disclaimer. Nobody associated with the production of this book hates women in general. There might be some hated people, and some of them may happen to be female, but that's about it. The amount of hate a person receives is not limited or otherwise influenced by the form and function of their genitalia. The author would like to stress, however, that the amount of love a person receives from him may indeed be traced directly to certain physical attributes, and these persons are exclusively women, so if there is an alleged bias it is towards the female sex and not against it.

Will this help prevent getting called "sexist misogynist chauvinist scum" by certain individuals? No.

But there are people out there that need to be aware that this is not about them. This is about feminists. Not people who think they're feminists. A distinction which initially is hard to make when one grew up with egalitarian beliefs and being told that these are equal to feminism. We will discover the roots of this ideology, sprouted in the twisted minds of few, a sect like Jim Jones' *Peoples Temple* – just that many are unaware of the bigger plans, just doing what they're told, willingly handing out poison, believing it's lemonade.

Tough comparison? Surely.

A tribute to Margaret Thatcher? Possibly.

The destructive forces she so pointedly described are still at work. They are walking amongst us, wearing the corpse of a loved one to lure us in, to pretend to be one of us. Well - considering that cancer is a part of the host's body, they might actually be.

The body referred to herein is the West - the part of the world that shows best what happens when society implements feminism instead of egalitarianism. May it serve as an example for developing nations not to make the same mistakes and as a wake-up call for those here already suffering the devastating effects. These are the waters we will navigate. Hold on tight when we travel through time to the beginnings of mankind, visit the Middle Ages and get off the ride in modern times to take a good hard look around. We will discover lies and deception, and the reasons behind them. We will understand some mechanics of society, and our eyes will be opened to what waits ahead.

Better the devil you know, they say. So cling to this little boat, tie yourself to the mast, and don't be afraid to get wet - you're in for a bumpy ride.

The Stone Age

For our first stop we couldn't go much further back in time if we want to understand human society. It's the so called Stone Age. Men climbed down from the trees – and then helped women down. We can assume that it was this point in time when the female nagging started. Masses of disgusting insects and worms, stepping on sharp rocks, and, worst of all, getting sand into their vaginas. The latter a condition which, at least for feminists, still persists up to today.

But of course there also were real, more serious problems for early mankind. Hunting for food was often dangerous; anyone who ever found himself armed with nothing but a pointy stick in front of a raging wounded mammoth knows what I'm talking about. But what can you do when the woman is hungry and nags? On the bright side, countless men found eternal peace on those hunts.

Those who survived had to carry massive amounts of meat and fur and bones over large distances to get it to their caves. The wounded often died, since the only available medical treatment was praying to the sun god, which usually yielded less than stellar results. And when you finally made it home, you may found that another clan just invaded and you had to fight them to get your cave and woman back.

Not that women had it much easier. Diseases affected everyone, and so did the weather. A cold, long winter had devastating effects on the population, and especially on women, whose cold feet got engraved into their DNA and can still be felt today. Not all berries they gathered were edible, and some found out the hard way. To make up for all the losses, they had to be pregnant for quite an amount of time, actually, pretty much all the time. And though giving birth isn't quite the magical wonder modern people make it out to be, it was a dangerous endeavour as well. Many women died in childbirth or following infections, and their offspring had a hard time, too, as infant mortality was nothing like it is today.

So both genders had their different duties and hardships. Yes, some modern egalitarians may cry out that "gender" is a social construct, and to some degree it certainly is (though not as much as those people would like it). But how effective would a society be in which the wide-hipped, short-legged, weaker, mostly pregnant part of the clan went to hunt (risking additional injury and miscarriage for less yield), and the stronger, faster part stayed at the cave and collected fruits and firewood and tended to the kids?

That would be stupid.

Nonetheless, there are feminists that claim it was that way, because nothing would speak against it. **(Voss, 2013)** How they discard the biological arguments? They always cite the same: one or two lone observations of a chimpanzee subspecies and an indigenous tribe. Here, a group of chimpanzees has been observed to kill some smaller animals in tree holes, and the majority of this group was female – a clear hint that human females might have been hunters as well?

No. First, grabbing a small animal from a hole is rather collecting than hunting.

Second, the sexual dimorphism in humans is much more prominent than in chimpanzees. Which is a good thing, else women would spend hours removing all that excess body and facial hair and bra producers would have a very hard time.

Third, chimpanzees can't speak, contrary to human females, who would've scared away any prey with their constant nagging. Unless the hunting party was all women, then it would've been bitching that would've driven away even the largest mammoth.

Regarding those comparisons with chimps, I actually prefer the Bonobo one: Feminists like to cite them as an example for a matriarchy, ignoring that it's (relatively) peaceful only due to the constant sex the females are handing out, often in exchange for food, or just to keep everyone calm. Now, most men could live with that, unfortunately, as always, feminism only cites the part it likes, and having sex whenever men want would be oppression of women, of course.

But enough of apes - what about those indigenous peoples, in this case the Agta? Well, it is one small tribe among thousands in the world; even in their home region, the Philippines, there are more than hundred other tribes. Yet only those vanishingly small exception is taken as proof for a prehistoric rule. As if this wasn't ridiculous enough, even most of the Agta women have never heard of female hunters. Fewer than hundred Agta women have claimed to have ever hunted, and most of them said they stopped hunting before the time of the observation. Real data exists for only six women hunters. Six. It really needs a feminist to take those six women from the twentieth century and base a theory about all of prehistoric mankind on them. For the overwhelming majority of cultures, it's a completely different picture:

Table 1

Average Percentage of Male Participation in Activities in Societies From the Standard Cross-Cultural Sample

Predominantly masculine activities	Index (%)	Quasi-masculine activities	Index (%)	Swing activities	Index (%)	Quasi-feminine activities	Index (%)
Hunting large aquatic fauna	100	Butchering	92.3	Generation of fire	62.3	Fuel gathering	27.2
Smelting of ores	100	Collection of wild honey	91.7	Bodily mutilation	60.8	Preparation of drinks	22.2
Metalworking	99.8	Land clearance	90.5	Preparation of skins	54.6	Gathering of wild vegetal foods	19.7
Lumbering	99.4	Fishing	86.7	Gathering small land fauna	54.5	Dairy production	14.3
Hunting large land fauna	99.3	Tending large animals	82.4	Crop planting	54.4	Spinning	13.6
Work in wood	98.8	Housebuilding	77.4	Manufacture of leather products	53.2	Laundering	13.0
Fowling	98.3	Soil preparation	73.1	Harvesting	45.0	Water fetching	8.6
Making musical instruments	97.6	Netmaking	71.2	Crop tending	44.6	Cooking	8.3
Trapping	97.5	Making rope and cordage	69.9	Milking	43.8	Preparation of vegetal food	5.7
Boatbuilding	96.6			Basketmaking	42.5		
Stoneworking	95.9			Burden carrying	39.3		
Work in bone, horn, shell	94.6			Matmaking	37.6		
Mining and quarrying	93.7			Care of small animals	35.9		
Bonesetting	92.7			Preservation of meat or fish	32.9		
				Loom weaving	32.5		
				Gathering small aquatic fauna	31.1		
				Manufacture of clothing	22.4		
				Potterymaking	21.1		

Note. Data are from Tables 1–5 of "Factors in the Division of Labor by Sex: A Cross-Cultural Analysis," by G. P. Murdock and C. Provost, 1973, *Ethnology, 12,* pp. 207–210 Copyright 1973 by the University of Pittsburgh Press. Reprinted with permission. Each index represents the average percentage of male participation in each activity, as calculated by Murdock and Provost (1973) from 185 societies of the Standard Cross-Cultural Sample (Murdock & White, 1969). Each index was calculated for a given activity such that each society received a weight indicating whether the activity was exclusively male (1.0), predominantly male (0.8), equally performed by both sexes (0.5), predominantly female (0.2), or exclusively female (0). The weights were summed across societies in which the activity was performed and then divided by the number of societies. Murdock and Provost identified the four clusters of activities on the basis of this index and the variability in the index across geographic regions. The swing activities were more variable than the quasi-masculine or quasi-feminine activities, which were more variable than the strictly masculine ones

(Wood & Eagly, 2002)

Why do feminists feel the need to reinterpret history? Why are the female duties not respected? Even the cavemen valued their women, why can't feminists? Women always have contributed to society, the most valuable was the offspring. Collecting fruits and wood, caring for the children – they did their part for the survival of the race. Even if it's just through nagging; there's quite a chance that men climbed down the trees in the first place to get away from that.

Why is feminism ridiculing these contributions and only focusing on the male duties? It's almost as if they think women were worth less when they didn't do stuff that is considered male, which would put feminists on the same level with the worst misogynists. They probably are victims of the global conspiracy they call "the patriarchy", which only a small indigenous tribe managed to escape. The world would be a better place if they would just pack up and disappeared into the jungle.

But they don't.

Instead they try to rewrite history, especially the earliest history, which is convenient, since the only reliable accounts from back then are cave paintings and the occasional artifact (most of which are pretty sexist, though, with giant penises and large breasts and pregnant bellies). This brings us to a related myth from back then, or, more exact, a myth from nowadays that is projected back in time: "Women are the sexual selectors".

This is quite a dilemma. On first glance (and feminism hates nothing more than a deeper look) it seems to make sense: A woman puts some bug blood on her lips, rubs her armpits (and maybe a bit down there) with a peppermint plant, dresses in her best fur and throws herself on the market. What man could resist that? So she can choose her mate and get it on. But wait – which one does she choose? The successful alpha male, the leader of the clan or some other influential figure? Someone like a good hunter, well-built, obviously good genes? This would make sense, but if all the other women go by the same rules, wouldn't that make those alpha males the selectors? On the other hand, those males are driven by competition with other males, could this also be an instinct to appeal to women? To a degree, it sure is.

How do we sort this out? Let's make a test. We take the least desirable woman of the clan and have her select the most desirable man. How is she going to do that? There isn't much more she can do apart from showing off her secondary sex characteristics, in those days known as "gazongas" and developed for this reason, to attract males. But that's pretty passive, can't she do anything else? No. If the desired man doesn't fall for her, she's fucked – in our scenario, unfortunately for her, only figuratively.

Now we take the least desirable man of the clan and have him set his sights on the most desirable female. Chances are, she's doing it with the chief or some other big shot. What can he do about it? Not much, apart from arranging a hunting accident to make her an available widow, it seems … no, wait! He could simply rape her. If the chief is around or she rats him out, his life expectancy might drop sharply, but in those days it wasn't high to begin with, and at least he had a shot at getting her pregnant and thus pass on his genes. A pretty good shot even, as rape is twice as reliable as consensual sex to get the receiving female pregnant. **(Herzog, 2012)** Now, remember, we're not building a case for rape here. We just show that men have an active option to choose a sexual partner even against her will, and this would even result in a higher chance of pregnancy. Women have only limited and completely passive abilities to choose, and thus calling them "sexual selectors" is pretty far-fetched.

Almost as far as our next stop in time, the ancient world! How's that for a transition?

The Ancient World

We see the rise of civilization. Finally, the nagging of women can be recorded and finds its way into history (Xanthippe). People build legendary structures like the Seven Wonders of the World, and they also build social structures, hierarchies.

Surprisingly, unlike feminists want to make us believe, women were not at the bottom of it, at least not exclusively. Lines were drawn in society, but rather between rich and poor than between men and women. Those born into wealthy and influential families enjoyed a life in luxury, common people had to fight for survival and quite a bunch of people were enslaved. The latter men often ended up drafted and used as cheap soldiers to be slaughtered in a war or, like in Rome, as gladiators to risk their lives for entertainment purposes, while the female slaves became maids or sex toys. Now, the feminist narrative is pretty clear on this: to occasionally have sex is much, much worse than being torn apart by a lion.

Of course, some men ended up as sex toys for wealthy females as well. Women like Valeria Messalina got it on with half of Rome, untouchable due to her power and influence, women like Cleopatra ruled countries and made a sport of poisoning her slaves. Yet they were women, were supposed to be oppressed victims. Of course not all women became murdering whores, but those who strived for power often ended this way. It still were harsh times: disputes were often solved by force, and murder was a common shortcut to inheritances. And still the medical achievements were nothing compared to modern times, so for the common people to survive, the woman had to do a good share of birthing.

This even was their assigned duty in feminist paradises like Sparta. Often lauded as giving women equal rights, it had a clear distinction between the genders: The men were taking care of the military, the women of the household. For a man to have his name inscribed on his gravestone, he had to die in battle; for a woman to receive this honor, she had to die in childbirth. Of course this aspect is not touched upon very readily. It's the usual cherry-picking, it goes on and on – is your stomach already churning? I hope not, we still got quite a lot to digest, so let's hop right on to the next chapter.

The Middle Ages

In medieval times, the idolization of women reached a degree that can only be matched by our present. Women were pure creatures, almost untouchable, due partly to the rise of the church, that only allowed sex in the missionary position for the sole purpose of procreation and generally condemned lust, under which especially the men had to suffer. Also, the church revered the HOLY MOTHER OF GOD and provided education for girls as well as boys, even the poor, if they joined the cleric. Amongst them, there have been some more or less notable women, most just failed to leave a lasting impression, though.

This is one of the many Achilles' heels of feminism, and high heels at that. Some claim the lack of female contributions to advances in society is caused by keeping women from getting an education. Some (and quite often the same), however, will readily list influential and educated women when confronted with the assumption there never were such women. A capable rhetorician might enjoy putting those against each other or even get those two contradicting statements out of the same mouth. Of course, most of those "great women" were rarely heard of, since their contributions were rather insignificant; the real, likely cause of which we will examine later on, when we reach modern times.

So, again, women who were noble or born to a wealthy family enjoyed mostly the same benefits as their brothers, with the exception that the men went to see their teachers, while the women were visited by teachers mostly at home, as it was below a woman's dignity to run around town. Also, times were still not the best, violence was still highly present and frequent plagues decimated the ever increasing masses of people. Which means women were still needed to breed a lot, and that's what they did. And that's why they still were protected.

In fact, a whole culture evolved around the worshipping of women: Knights chose a princess and fought to the death for a handkerchief. Minnesinger travelled the lands and wrote poems and songs about beloved ladies. Great works of art were created in honor of women, which has been started back in ancient times with the Venus of Milo or even fertility figures in the Stone Age. Of course, such is denounced by feminists as "objectification of women", all the while men were busy breaking their backs when providing for their family or fighting off hordes of invading Arabs and Africans and Persians and even Mongols. It was still a physical world.

Of course feminists couldn't care less about the rest of mankind, all they are looking for is a reason to complain. Funnily enough, the women back then didn't complain; they surely still nagged from time to time, but they saw firsthand that being a man was not half as fun as modern feminists make it out to be. It's just now that there's talk about thousands of years of oppression. Maybe it satisfies those harpies to know that any halfway wealthy woman could have the male serfs whipped for oppressing her.

And with the sound of these lashes we hurry on. Do you still smell the sanitary catastrophe that was the Middle Ages? You will soon remember it fondly as we are approaching the foul stench of feminism.

It's already noticeable beneath the smoke of the factory chimneys that are rising now …

The Industrial Revolution

We're making progress. With the rise of machines and factories, the costs of products fell significantly and allowed better living standards and means of employment. With this newfound security, people of course got bored and had enough spare energy to complain about injustices.

With regards to feminism, this means the start of the "Women's Suffrage" movement, the fight to vote. Note that this wasn't called feminism (yet) and only later got reinterpreted as the first wave of feminism. Though the word already existed, coined by a French utopian, it wasn't widely known and was only used in the early twentieth century by a few radical women – *radical* being a word which really means something, considering the comparably moderate suffragettes didn't hesitate to attack people with axes and burn down houses.

Here we have to mention an important thing, which is that all those women fought for the universal right of women to vote, something not even men enjoyed. If a man belonged to the wrong confession, the wrong race or wasn't wealthy, he usually had no voting rights as well. On the other hand, there were women who could vote. Not only those associated with the church, where abbesses already voted in the church matters the same as men, while the general population was enslaved in serfdom. In Sweden, women voted as early as 1718. In the US, as early as 1756. Now we see the first glimpse of what lies ahead: A struggle for a right for all women which not even all men enjoyed – it wasn't about equal rights, it was about women's rights.

Of course, men fought for universal suffrage as well during the same time. Why should women get what they were denied? And both, men and women, succeeded. That is, generally they succeeded, since in a lot of places racial restrictions were still kept in place, so if your skin had the wrong color you still couldn't vote. But since a lot of feminists shared the opinion that black people weren't really people, it didn't really matter to them.

And with this, it was over. Women went to university, like Marie Curie in 1891, who even got a Nobel Prize in 1903. They could vote and get elected (like Jeannette Rankin in 1916 to the US Congress, or Nellie Ross in 1924 as governor). Women had the same rights; the highest honors in academia, the highest positions in politics – everything was available to them.

It could have ended there.

It should have ended there.

But it didn't.

There is no happy end to this story. Instead, from then on, everything took a turn for the worse.

The Second Wave

"The blood-dimmed tide is loosed, and everywhere
The ceremony of innocence is drowned;
The best lack all conviction, while the worst
Are full of passionate intensity."
(William Butler Yeats, "The Second Coming")

Though women weren't dependant on men anymore and could reach highest positions, most failed to do so. This was okay for most women, since they just did what they wanted to do. But feminists were enraged. Was this what their radical terrorist grandmothers fought for?

A good part of this rage was fueled by books like "The Natural Superiority of Women" by Ashley Montagu (born Israel Ehrenberg), which made rather ridiculous statements like: Women produce eggs, so they are essential to the future. Of course they do, but left to their own devices (i.e. eggs), they'd die out just the same as men. What Montagu plays on here is the old sociological perception of the disposability of men. One man can impregnate a thousand women and be father of at least a thousand children, and even much more in the span of his life. One woman can only bear a good dozen; so for a society, there need to be many women, but only a few men would suffice to ensure survival. That made women a valuable good, and since they're weaker and slower, there was a need to protect them from hardships in the past. But on a closer look, it appears questionable to assume some kind of "superiority" to women, especially, when the same developments that enabled women to be less dependent on men actually decreased their worth. Less women died in childbirth or due to diseases or violent conflicts, society already provided a safe environment, and women became abundant. We will later take another look back at this obsolete argument and see how modern feminism decreased the sociological value of women even more.

Montagu makes more ridiculous statements, for example that women have a stronger constitution and are thus the stronger sex – constitutionally. We see the same attempts of focusing on a single (and utterly irrelevant) trait to assume a general superiority, while ignoring the fact that actual strength was what ruled the world and keeps on ruling it in less developed civilizations – and even in modern ones, as soon as the framework gets shaken by catastrophes. It doesn't even need a war or a natural catastrophe like an earthquake or a flooding; a simple prolonged power blackout might be enough to melt away the sugarcoating of modern civilization and have women find themselves in need of protection again.

Montagu also realizes this and claims that "technology frees up women to be as strong or stronger than men", since "you do not have to be physically strong to hold a gun". Let's disregard the cheap trick of asserting "natural superiority" by making up for natural *inferiority* through the use of *technology*. Now, I can see how women can use a forklift the same as a man; but how does this somehow make them stronger? This would require technology that can be exclusively used by women, and unless there are estrogen-activated machines, it's safe to say that a man can use machines and weapons just as good as any woman – if not better. Male testosterone levels have been shown key to superior spatial ability in men, so understanding the three-dimensional environment would give men the advantage in operating machines, including weaponry. You do not only need to hold the gun, you need to be able to shoot and hit your target.

The rather martial example with the gun doesn't come from nowhere. Feminists are fascinated, if not obsessed, with strength and power, and subsequently with inflicting corporal harm to their enemies: Men. Disappointed in the general female population, who still regarded men favorable, more efforts had to be undertaken to not only make women aware of their "superiority", but also to make them view men as their enemies as well.

To achieve this objective, more man-hating "literature" was created by feminists, sometimes under male pen names (like James Tiptree). Naturally, it was mostly in the genre of science fiction – as we have seen, feminists like to blur the lines between science and fiction to further their cause. And boy, did they envision gynotopias! Men enslaved and dominated, kept as slaves and pets, killed off by accidental viruses or ones specifically engineered for this purpose, or just outright murdered by women. That's right, the message is clear: kill all men and the world will be a better place. Now imagine something like this but arguing for the extermination of women, or another race. Disgusting fantasies, you say? But if it's feminist, it will even get awards and be praised, like Joanna Russ' "The Female Man".

In those works of science fiction we see a pattern that will continue from then on, not only in mixing and replacing facts with fantasy, but also that men are acceptable targets for such violent dreams. "The Female Man" was nominated for an award in 1975, but it actually won two awards in 1996 and 2002. So don't think that it was just some kind of temporary mood that made this acceptable, this has become a mainstream attitude.

Dangerous ground, you say?

It is. Since those ideas didn't stay in the realm of fiction.

In 1967, Valerie Solanas, a feminist with a degree in psychology, published the "SCUM Manifesto", a rather disturbing rant against men with a simple solution: Kill them all (SCUM is an acronym standing for Society for Cutting Up Men, as found on the cover of her first self-published edition). Of course some more moderate feminists tried to play it down as a parody, but shortly after publishing her manifesto, Solanas went on and shot Andy Warhol and another man, then tried to kill another but her gun jammed. Solanas thought herself to be the victim of a conspiracy. Of course, the "patriarchy" struck back with all its male force and not only diagnosed her with paranoid schizophrenia but also made her serving a three year sentence, partially in a psychiatric hospital. Inhuman, isn't it? No wonder women are outraged at such mistreatment.

There are several lessons learned from this.

First, just like the axe-throwing, arson-loving furies many decades earlier, human life doesn't mean anything to feminists, at least as long as it's male.

Second, just because someone has a degree in a "social science" like psychology doesn't mean they are in any way reliable or even sane.

Third, "the patriarchy" is as much a conspiracy theory as anything else made up by paranoid schizophrenics.

Obviously, feminists succeeded in suppressing these simple truths. How did they achieve that, you ask? Well, they aren't that dumb to believe an openly violent confrontation as envisioned by Russ, Solanas and others could actually be won by women. Not unless men were reduced to, say, ten percent of the population, something feminist Sally Miller Gearhart proposed in her essay "The Future – If There Is One – Is Female" to ensure a world entirely dominated by women. For this to happen, women had to be brought into positions of power. But how could this be done when many women still preferred family life to a life of studying and working? Well, the first step was to make university more appealing to women and offer other courses besides all that dry stuff. Let's invent some new academic fields, preferably such where people can't be wrong due to various possibilities of interpretation. Born was the notorious Women's Studies. A place for women to talk about women, about being women, and about what pigs men are. Well, the latter might not be mentioned that directly, but just to give you a clue about what was being done here: One of the first to teach women's studies was Sally Miller Gearhart. Yes, that's right, Mrs. Ten Percent spread her wisdom to countless young women. It should also be noted that she was a lesbian, like many feminists of that time, which may help to explain the rampaging hatred for men in those circles and the often rather shortsighted fantasies about eliminating all males.

These lesbian murder-glorifying paranoid schizophrenic women gave birth to feminism. And they got themselves into positions that enabled them to spread their hatred.

The Sixties and Seventies of the last century saw the struggle of the black man for equal rights. As we remember, when women got their rights together with indigent men, racial prejudice still ran high among women's activists, and black people were excluded from gaining these rights. Now that those people rose up to claim the same rights, feminists saw a chance to continue their way to world domination, a just cause in their eyes as the superiority of women had been "proven" by Montagu, a view most of the more lesbian oriented feminists shared with a passion. All they had to do was hijacking the sense of injustice created by the black power movement, to surf that same wave of compassion. Women are still victims, too!

History got reinterpreted. The dependence of women on men got spun to have been "oppression", even though women would've had no chance of surviving in the physical worlds of the past where men competed. These worlds haven't been unfair to women – they've been unfair to the weak. But of course that wasn't possible for feminists to acknowledge, as they held the firm belief of female superiority. Thanks, Montagu!

And so the battle of the sexes was declared.

Not a physical battle, for obvious reasons, but a hidden battle which began with the poisoning of the youth. Feminists infiltrated the education sector. Traditionally, there were always a lot of female teachers, and now those got indoctrinated or replaced by feminists. After all, a degree in Women's Studies doesn't give you many possibilities on the job market aside from, well, teaching Women's Studies. Young girls got told that they were superior, that men are oppressors, that there is a war on women, and a battle of the sexes is raging.

Men had become enemies.

If a woman didn't feel like dying of radiation like Marie Curie, she could now blame male oppression for it. "Surely I would have a Nobel by now, too, if it weren't for the patriarchy keeping me down!"

And the patriarchy's arm is a long one. It reaches right into the smallest unit of oppression, the family. Getting married, maybe even getting pregnant, was made out to be male tyranny. The only way for a women to be truly free was to avoid men and go her own way, and maybe becoming lesbian along the way, which would be a side effect many of the lesbian teachers welcomed. You think I was just joking with the last sentence? Not quite. As Alison

Jaggar stated in *Feminist Politics and Human Nature*: "[The nuclear family is] a cornerstone of woman's oppression: it enforces women's dependence on men, it enforces heterosexuality [...]" Yes, you got that right, heterosexuality was reinterpreted to be oppression as well.

Robin Morgan wrote in *Sisterhood is Powerful*: "We can't destroy the inequities between men and women until we destroy marriage."

The famous Simone de Beauvoir made quite clear how much of a choice young women should have in their lives: "No woman should be authorized to stay at home and raise her children. Society should be totally different. Women should not have that choice, precisely because if there is such a choice, too many women will make that one." **(de Beauvoir, 1975)**

This left only one course of action:

The traditional family had to be abolished.

And feminists found a mighty ally: capitalists.

Wealthy entrepreneurs like the Rockefellers supported the feminist ideology. The motive is pretty clear: Destroying the traditional family will massively boost the economy. There will be no sharing of the same bed anymore, instead the bed industry will sell two beds, one to the man and one to the woman. Getting men and women living separate lives was a highly profitable strategy, more than enough to pay the new female workforce, especially since the increased competition among workers gave employers the upper hand when negotiating salaries – especially with the bright outlook of increasing automation on the horizon. And as earlier studies in marketing had shown (women publicly smoking, sold to them as an act of liberation by the tobacco industry), women were great consumers, easily influenced and paying more for shiny things. Also, another fly was squatted with the same strike: Feminism helped to transform the age-old oppression of the poor by the rich, which was under attack by the hippie movement, into a perceived oppression of women by men. Suddenly, selling yourself to capitalism became a right to fight for, something to strive for. With this, capitalism was able to gain unprecedented credibility and, of course, profits.

The capitalists weren't the only ones who profited. The government now could look forward to have double the tax payers. I can't speculate on the six-figure sum Gloria Steinem received from the CIA, I don't want to accidentally touch the truth and go missing. But it may be clear that the government had reasons to support even the more cynical aspects of feminism.

So the only losers were men and women, but women at least felt liberated (ignoring that they had all the possibilities for more than fifty years already).

They got freed, in a way: from the role of

being a mother. In more than one way. Along came the pill.

Of course this was a big feminist issue, since having babies automatically meant that the affected woman was being oppressed and robbed of her freedom. In a way this train of thought takes some blame from men, since getting pregnant couldn't be helped in past millennia, and the pill just arrived in modern times; but since feminists are women after all, they still blame men. We also shouldn't forget that the more radical feminists still consider any kind of sexual intercourse rape and oppression, even to this day, so that may explain the rather weird approaches to this topic.

They also fought to legalize abortions for those women who forgot to take the pill. An array of possibilities to make women into that what they should be: workers, not mothers.

All this summed up in the more positive term of "reproductive rights", to which we will dedicate a later chapter, since there's much to say about that.

In the meantime, let's take a break and get a drink, to wash away the bad taste all that feminism left in our mouths. Better take the bottle with you, since it won't get better anytime soon.

On the contrary.

The Story So Far ...

As we've seen, it was a harsh world, those recent several thousand years. Men and women evolved physically and mentally for different duties in a society that regarded women as valuable ("women and children first") and men as rather disposable. Those with power ruled the poor. When industry and medicine made life considerably less of a challenge, the "Women's Lib" movement was born, along (but not together with) movements of disenfranchised men to challenge the rule of powerful men and women. They succeeded and everybody enjoyed the same freedom.

That wasn't enough. Blinded by delusions of superiority, feminism was born in an unholy alliance of femdom fetishists, bloodthirsty writers, man-hating lesbians, manipulating capitalists, greedy politicians and outright insane women. Programs were created to push women into all areas of life and support them by all means necessary. The traditional way of life, even traditional intercourse was portrayed as oppression, signs of a conspiracy to keep women down. Everything was done to rile up women against men and destroy the family. Feminists who advocated a reduction of the male population to "manageable" proportions, even feminists who advocated the murder of men altogether, became teachers and their works became taught in schools and universities. An unprecedented wave of hate in the name of "freedom" started to poison the minds of young people. Girls were told that they needed to destroy this "man's world" that oppressed women. Ironically, feminism aimed to take away what made women female, namely giving birth and raising children, and rather tried to make them into workers and, by extension, men. Maybe this just shows that this ideology was heavily influenced by mentally ill women, or maybe it's a sign for how much influence the capitalists had on the movement, but feminism oriented itself on male values. They felt treated unjust in a "patriarchy" and aimed to destroy it by becoming a part of it and competing within its rules. Women changed to become like men, and only destroyed their own (biologically assigned) former part in society. Of course a true feminist would claim this shows to what immense degree women are victims of the patriarchy, even feminism itself. That's the other emerging pattern, a fluent transition between claiming superiority and pretending to be a victim; a ridiculous game which will be seen in the next chapter about the "wage gap".

At this point of time, millions of women listen to Nancy Sinatra and get brainwashed in

"Women's Studies" and "Gender Relations" courses, and then, surprisingly, can't find a job in these fields despite splendid grades and trickle into media, politics and back into education to further the legends of "the patriarchy" discriminating against women and denying them a job where they can just sit and complain. About what, when all the issues were resolved long, long ago? Well, there are two issues that became kind of cornerstones, the last covers that are never to be blown, else people would realize what feminism really is about, which would spell the end of feminism.

These two issues are the so-called "wage gap" and women's "reproductive rights", two issues closely related as we will see. Let's take a look at the first.

The Wage Gap Myth

Whenever a feminist gets under pressure and needs to explain exactly how they are victims in modern society, they claim that women are discriminated against in the workplace. Despite thousands of programs (and billions of dollars that are poured into those programs) to get women into all kinds of jobs, they earn less than men. Even nowadays. That's an outrage!

Unless we actually look at the situation a little closer.

While women were not caring that much for their jobs and instead often still got married and pregnant and raised kids, when they got into the workplace, they of course were a risk for their employer. Before the widespread availability of the pill, reliable birth control was non-existent. Even if they started off at the same pay, when they began raising kids and worked only part-time or quit and returned to work in later years, they shockingly didn't earn as much as the men who spent their lives consistently on that job and had time to work on their career – full-time. This isn't a joke; feminists complain that women earn less, even when the reason for this "scandal" lies in the simple fact that women work less. **(FAZ, 2012)**

But why do women choose more family-friendly jobs? Because biology lures them with female instinct? Nope, it's because they are brainwashed by the patriarchy.

Writes Christina Hoff Sommers in *Wage Gap Myth Exposed – By Feminists*:

"According to the National Organization for Women (NOW), powerful sexist stereotypes 'steer' women and men 'toward different education, training, and career paths' and family roles. But are American women really as much in thrall to stereotypes as their feminist protectors claim? Aren't women capable of understanding their real preferences and making decisions for themselves? NOW needs to show, not dogmatically assert, that women's choices are not free. And it needs to explain why, by contrast, the life choices it promotes are the authentic ones – what women truly want, and what will make them happier and more fulfilled." **(Sommers, 2012)**

Remember the second wave? How women had to be forced out of family, how family life was reinterpreted as oppression and leading feminists said women should have no choice? Those ideologies are alive and kicking, even today, and not in the minds of some backward fanatics, but in the National Organization of Women and other official institutions with massive political influence (well, let's not forget the possibility that they could be comprised of backward fanatics).

Of course there will always be some incurable women who, at some point in their lives, leave work for some amount of time in order to get kids. Which means in the grand total of the population, women are prone to end up earning less than men, at least unless men get anywhere close to being awarded similar custody rates.[1] Which in turn means, feminists can continue to spin the statistics to play the victim card – the only way to earn the same while working less would be if women actually earned more. The first demographic to show such trend, the first step on the way, would be women who work the same as men but earn more than them.

And that's exactly what's happening.

Young, unmarried women without children earn eight percent more on average than their male colleagues. This gets even worse in big cities: In New York, it's 17 percent, in Los Angeles 12 percent. **(Alfonsi, 2010)**

You think that's unfair? Think again. Suddenly, feminists are full of excuses for this imbalance. Suddenly, it's not discrimination or a

---

[1] This is quite unlikely due to the feminist propaganda of women being able to "have it all": They celebrate the fact that women don't need a man and can work and have a "family" on their own; either by having the man paying support or by letting a random guy impregnate them and then get the support from the government. Of course, as a single mom ("strong, independent woman"), they are even more prone to work less, due to the additional strain.

systematic preference of women. No, it's because women deserve to earn more, because they work harder, because they negotiate better - everything feminists dismissed in explanations why men earned (or for some, still are *perceived* to earn) more, is now an acceptable argument when it's women who profit from it. Because women are "superior" workers. **(Ackerman, 2013)** Yes, the thought of female superiority is still around as well, did you think otherwise? No, it gets perpetuated over and over again.

Though it also should be notes that wages in general, at least for men, have been stagnant since the mid-Seventies, they should by now be twice as much as they are. Since the same time (the high time of the *Second Wave* that flushed millions of women into the job market) the profits of the top 1% increased to the highest levels ever. **(Sorscher, 2011)**

Forty years of supporting women (and only women), forty years of massive lobbying, forty years of twisting statistics, of media onslaught and pressing companies into hiring more women, raising the salaries of women and promoting more women finally paid off. Feminism created a society in which being a woman is enough to get freebies at every corner while men have to work harder than ever. And that's okay! Feminists even use this skewed system as justification for sex selection in favor of girls – parents realize that girls have much better chances in this new feminist paradise. **(Rosin, 2010)**

Yes, the US is going the same way as some third world countries that were preferring boys and were heavily condemned by feminists for doing so. Now that the same is happening the other way round, it is praised.

Won't somebody please think of the children? Feminists do, but only if the children are female.

Which brings us to the next big issue of feminism.

Reproductive Rights

Since feminism is about control, this naturally includes birth control. It includes especially birth control, since those "reproductive rights" are almost exclusively for women. The only non-surgical way for men to "control" reproduction is the use of a condom, and it comes at the price of reduced sensitivity. Unsurprisingly, the lesbian feminists don't care, as for them the most preferable solution would be men having no sex whatsoever with women (we remember: heterosexuality is oppression). Women, on the other hand, have plenty of contraceptives, and of course the main weapon in the arsenal: Abortion. Ultimately, it's the woman's decision – and only hers -, if there will be a child or not. It's another important sign that feminism is not about equal rights. If it were, feminists would either drop all abortion campaigns, so women had the same measures as men (contraceptives), or they would fight to include men in the process to determine if an abortion should be approved or denied, as it is his offspring as well. But no, feminists fight to have those rights exclusively for women.

And how should they use them?

We already read from those feminists that

endorse sex selection in favor of girls, which rings eerily familiar when we think of those early Women's Studies teachers demanding the reduction of men to approximately ten percent of the population. The echoes of those morbid fantasies can still be heard nowadays, not only in the rather careful sex selection endorsements, but also in the more outright demands of "abort the males!" **(Heflin, 2012)**

Well, they have to reach the ten percent mark somehow, don't they?

Many will dismiss them as radical, fanatic – but that's what feminism is. An ideology based on hateful nutjobs. For them, it's not a reproductive right, it's also a weapon to get rid of (or at least dominate) men.

Though it might be questionable if men would just accept such "gendercide" when it really became an issue, instead of just calling it a day and ending the failed experiment of giving women extended rights there and then. Thankfully, those feminists are still a long way from achieving their objectives, though it is disturbing how willfully the mainstream media furthers their goals and gives them a public forum to spread their hatred.

But most women are blissfully unaware of those darker intentions and don't even realize how skewed all the reproductive rights are in their favor. A simple comparison:

Scenario A

Woman: "Hey, let's have sex, but don't come in me."

Man: "Alright."

Things get steamy, and – whoops! – he comes inside her.

He can now be prosecuted for rape, since she didn't give consent to that part of sex, the woman can take the morning-after pill, get an abortion or get the kid and have the man pay child support for the next decades.

Scenario B

Man: "Hey, you sure I don't need a condom? I don't want kids."

Woman: "Yeah, I'm on the pill, don't worry."

Turns out she lied and gets pregnant, but the man will have to pay even though he didn't consent to procreation.

You will only ever hear about the first scenario from feminists when it comes to reproductive rights. Generally, rape is the favorite word of feminists, as it shows the oppressive nature of (heterosexual) intercourse. Another scenario you will never hear about is a man wanting to be a father and have a child, and the woman aborting anyway. That seems cruel. The cruelty would only be pointed out when a woman wants to have a kid and the man doesn't, and he would demand an abortion - the horror! It's the usual double standard we can expect from the feminist narrative. They even fight a much lesser alternative: that a man could have the right to abort his duty to pay, in the same way the woman has the right to abort the baby altogether.

One of the landmark court decisions in this regard was *Dubay v. Wells* (in which a woman told the man she was infertile and on birth control, then became pregnant and promptly sued for child support), during which was remarkably stated that the state has "the power to treat different classes of persons in different ways". **(Clay, Gibbons, & Hood, 2007)**

Not much about equality here, and yet (better: therefore) feminists celebrated when it was ruled that men had to pay. They usually argue that the duty only arises when the child is already born, and the woman only has the right to abort before it is born. However, it would be easy to implement laws that give the father the same time-frame as the woman to either opt in or out, and the woman could base her decision for a real abortion on it. They also ignore the fact that a woman still has options to get rid of the child even after birth, either by giving it up for adoption or dropping it off at a "safe haven" (e.g. USA) or a "baby hatch" (e.g. Germany). Fun Fact: Until 2008, the laws in Nebraska allowed for any child under 18 to be dropped off. The first child that was given away was a 11-year-old boy, and later kids have been as old as 17. **(Knapp, 2008)**

Now, if that wasn't convenient for mothers! They can get rid of their responsibilities even after birth – men can't. And yet feminists complain men would want to "control their reproductive rights" – when all men want is just a fraction of those rights. Men don't even want to kill the kids. Which, by the way, many women also see as a viable solution, even after birth, as they are more than twice as likely than fathers to kill their offspring. In 2011, around 80 percent of all child fatalities were killed by their parents. Of those, a little over 20 percent involved both parents; of the remaining, 17 percent died with only the father participating, in 39,4 percent was only the mother involved. **(United States Children's Bureau, 2012)**

As we see, women have absolute control over the reproductive process of all men, and feminists fight hard to keep it that way. They don't want to share any of it, as this would be a step towards equal rights – and that's not what feminism is about.

On a funny and frightening note, the scientific advance relating to artificial wombs is thus regarded anxiously by feminists, even though it would make women more available for the job market. At the same time, the old argument "it's my body" wouldn't count anymore, and men might actually get equal rights. Also, the ever-repeated "men are unnecessary" mantra might then get an adequate response. One argument shows the mindset of a typical feminist in a great way:

'There are going to be real problems,' said organiser Dr Scott Gelfand, of Oklahoma State University. 'Some feminists even say artificial wombs mean men could eliminate women from the planet and still perpetuate our species. That's a bit alarmist. Nevertheless, this subject clearly raises strong feelings.' **(McKie, 2002)**

Remember the Sci-Fi-fantasies of feminist writers about waging war against men and killing them all? Remember the paranoid-schizophrenic writings of Valerie Solanas in her SCUM Manifesto? The proposals of reducing men to a tiny minority? All these are still in the heads of feminists, this is the world they are living in, and of course they project their own delusions on the enemy and expect "the patriarchy" to actually wage the "war on women" they like to imagine.

Of course they are hysterical, but who will slap them and tell them to calm down? Nobody. Thanks, "Violence Against Women Act"! Instead they are allowed to roam freely and spread their poison and sink deeper into their madness.

The Third Wave

Now that we know the true goals of feminism, we won't be fooled by the decoys of those two age-old "issues" (of which one has become the contrary situation and one never was about equal rights). But even those who fall for it will need some variation on the old themes or they get bored, especially when they subconsciously feel that most of what they are told is bogus. A young western woman, who has been growing up with benefits that are unmatched by any other demographic group on the planet, will not feel oppressed enough. The invention of feminist disciplines in education has pumped out millions of feminists that need to further their goals, and though some (the most dangerous, probably) end up in politics or become feminist teachers themselves, most join the media. And it shows.

Within recent decades, since the second wave gained traction, a new "phenomenon" arose: man-bashing. It's not really that phenomenal; anyone knowing the origins, objectives and mindsets of feminists is hardly surprised. Feminists live in a constant war, and, knowing their physical disadvantage, rely heavily on psychological warfare. This goes as far as calling men "a disease" in a headline of the biggest German (and thus one of Europe's biggest) news magazine **(Blech & von Bredow, 2003)** or laughing and joking on daytime US TV about a man who got his penis cut off by his wife **(Hughes, 2011)**. Could anyone imagine the public outrage if women were targeted in such a way? The media, NGO and politicians would be all over this. But since this is about men – silence.

Well, this is entertaining for feminists, and it serves to traumatize little boys who, in our information age and due to afternoon TV, of course will be aware of it. But in order to appear still relevant, feminism also has to invent some new things from time to time. The so-called "third wave" came with some nice additions to the arsenal.

For one, it made the "privilege" argument wildly popular. Since there is a patriarchy pulling all the strings and oppressing women, being a man is a privilege. Everything is easier (though women get considerably more help through education and employment programs), men are respected (though men are constantly ridiculed and attacked in media and entertainment) and since men are so blinded by their awesome lives, they can't see or understand the women's struggle. If you don't see the oppression, you are either a man or a woman who was brainwashed by the patriarchy;

both warps your perception and thus you think there is no oppression. The convenient part is, this automatically renders any argument from a man invalid. If you are privileged, you cannot have a valid opinion on anything concerning the allegedly unprivileged groups. Which also makes any attempt at arguing that actually it's women who are privileged in our society pointless. They are not. It just seems that way to privileged people.

Apart from that, criticizing women is generally a bad idea, since it's pretty easy to get branded a "misogynist", which is even worse than being privileged. I guess.

Another achievement is the re-definition of fun. Remember the good old times when a man and a woman met at a bar on a Saturday night, both had a few drinks, than crashed at his or her place and did the old in'n'out? Well, that's rape now. Or, according to feminists, has always been. Remember – feminists? Those that damned heterosexuality? Those who consider any PIV (Penis In Vagina – I'm not even making that up, it's a feminist term) to be rape and oppression? It comes as no surprise that they not only destroyed this fun pastime by claiming that, as soon as the woman is intoxicated, she is unable to legally consent to the intercourse (which makes said intercourse rape). They also showed their usual double standard: The woman is not responsible for her consensual participation, it doesn't count. The man, however, is responsible for having sex with her, sorry: for raping her. It doesn't even matter if she does all the work herself and slams it in – it's always the penetrating part that does the raping, the penetrated is always the victim.

That's why in a feminist's perfect world, there is no penetration involved. Unless they use certain tools, but let's not go there.

We also saw the introduction of birth rape, which is any act of penetration with anything during birth, if the mother does not explicitly consent. Usually done by doctors, they probably have to get yet another insurance; against accidentally becoming rapists.

Rape is always a rewarding topic for feminists, as it portrays men as aggressors, women as victim, it demonizes sexual inter-course in the process – jackpot. By making as many situations as possible "rape", they can also claim to be relevant. I mean, it's not like there are laws against rape or anything. No, feminism has to fight "the patriarchy's" "rape culture". For the same act, men get thrown in jail and women get pitied as victims – if you don't see the oppression of women here, you're obviously privileged.

This "privilege" nonsense was also quickly picked up by other groups who claimed to be oppressed even more than women, especially transsexual and asexual and pansexual and genderfluid and transethnic and even transspecies persons (though I'm not sure if it's politically correct to describe the latter as "persons").

The attention people can get when claiming oppression led to some more outlandish claims. A middle-aged white male (the ultimate enemy for all of the groups, as those have the highest "privileges") could claim to be a black disabled lesbian girl on the inside. He could also claim to be a goldfish, but that wouldn't enrage feminists that much. The ghosts they called started to haunt them. It got even worse, as some postmodern egalitarians declared all gender identity a social construct: a theory that people got a physical sex, a body, but all the behavioral patterns were learned through society.

Now there's an interesting aspect which explains why some feminists actually got behind that theory. If they somehow could manage to make this point of view mainstream, it would enable them to avoid the inevitable backlash would they try to implement the original feminist goals of total control – nobody could talk about discrimination of men or "gendercide" when gender wouldn't exist. The modern "privilege" approach (women can't be sexist against men, blacks can't be racist against whites) would be taken a notch further: men can't be discriminated against their gender, because "men" and "women" don't exist anymore. If feminists would gain control of society, any preference for (biological) women would therefore not be discrimination, just coincidence.

Naturally, a lot of feminists disagree on that, as it would hurt their belief of female superiority. They could drop the mask later on, but meanwhile run the risk that true egalitarians get to power and feminism is abolished in the process. These egalitarians get support especially from the transpeople community, as their sex-change operations might become obsolete, as there might be easier ways to just re-program their internal gender to match the body, not the other way around. It would also provide help for those believing they are goldfish trapped in the body of humans.

However, closer looks seem to expose those theories as rather baseless, anyway. For some insight into the whole "nature vs. nurture" debate, it is recommended to watch a Norwegian documentary series called "Hjernevask" – "Brainwash". It is available for free on the internet, with English subtitles, and will provide not only a much-needed, fact-based counterpoint to those theories of modern "social sciences", the reactions of some of those "scientists" also superbly show their train of thought. If you think science should tell you facts, think again. Science should tell you how to think, regardless of facts. An approach that only became relevant when feminism invaded the scientific community.

In the Middle Ages, the church dictated what was made known to the people. In the 21st century, we have the media and "social scientists" volunteering for the role as moral watchdog.

But since that only concerns some parts of feminism, let's get back to the main business!

War of Words

Feminism interprets society as a "battle of the sexes". "War against men" might thus be the more appropriate term, but since feminists are pretty good in propaganda (there's no feasible other way for them to fight), they try to hide their aggression and instead blame men by distorting history into an "oppression" by men. As easily history could be interpreted as a rule of women: Women leisurely stayed at home while the men had to work in horrible, often dangerous conditions, to bring her money and food – like a slave. For obvious reasons feminists don't do that.

Also for less obvious reasons, as their capitalist sponsors want to portray any kind of labor as liberation. In order to cater to those allies, feminists are always eager to prove the usefulness of women to them, which also serves as another point to show the dominance of women to the rest of the population. For example, there are several studies cited from time to time which show that in partnerships, 80% of buying decisions are influenced by women. It may be interesting to point out the choice of words: "influenced" – not "made by". Now, if a couple talks about a purchase, it already counts as influence. Just as easy it could be spun the other way round (men also influence a majority of buying decisions), but that's a road feminists don't want to go. If they did, it would only be said to be another sign of oppression: men forcing their opinions onto women. But that would make women lose the support of the industry and marketing, and especially the latter is imperative, as it influences the public perception of women. Commercials have to show strong women and pathetic men, to please the relevant target group. For this PR, feminists do not shy away from playing with words to exaggerate (we don't want to call it lying, now, do we?). Heck, in those buying decision studies they often even include purchases made by single men, with woman *indirectly* involved, for example deodorants or cars, when surveys show men consider their choice's appeal to women.

But how are feminists able to spread this misinformation? Surely journalists have an interest in reporting the truth!

Just kidding, of course. We all know how it works.

The first claims that were spread were that women consume more media than men, so the networks knew whom to appease. Apart from that, the left holds a traditionally high percentage of media jobs, and feminism is one of their pets.[2] And let's not forget the millions of women who got into university and did their Women's Studies, all too eager to write enthusiastic blogs and concert efforts to edit Wikipedia so they can put a feminist spin on things. **(Al Jazeera, 2013)** A few recovered, but unstoppable indoctrinated masses flooded onto the job market each year and ended up in the media. It's safe to say that the media has been, since the Seventies, thoroughly infiltrated by feminists who by now often hold positions of power in the news networks, so it's not getting better anytime soon.

Examples for this are abundant. Thousands and thousands of studies that are published and always have one thing in common: they are favorable for women. Statistics that show women are better drivers (even when they include accidents in motorsports, where women are an absolute minority, or studies done in a parking garage comparing women using the easily accessible women's parking area to the rest),; generally baseless claims that women are better in suffering pain (when it's easy to find

---

[2] Just like racism. The strategy is always the same, for both sides: Tell a group of people that others are out to get them. The right traditionally uses geographic, national borders. The left draws the borders right through society in general, separating men and women, black and white. In the end it's only about creating a problem out of thin air and then promise to address it in order to get votes.

dozens of studies to the contrary, though these are usually only published in medical journals and rarely hit the mainstream media, which should come as no surprise); some really funny stuff how men are closer related to chimpanzees than women. Take a look at the last one: A good feminist "study" comparing men to male chimps and women to male chimps, and finding that the male human has more in common with the male chimp than the female human. **(RP, 2012)** Now, of course one could've done it the other way round: Compare a woman to a female chimp and a man to a female chimp. But to conclude that women are closer to chimps than men? No way. This example is even more remarkable in its audacity when we consider that scientists found that the part of the human genes that differs the most from chimpanzees is – the y-chromosome. **(NBC/AP, 2010)** Of course the scientists were quick to add that this doesn't necessarily mean that women are less evolved. Such a disclaimer is mandatory, because without it, such findings would most certainly not be reported. A courtesy which men can not expect when it's the other way round.

A great example in 2012 was the study of James R. Flynn, which was reported all over the world in all big, medium and small media to show that women had surpassed men in intelligence. What happened? James Flynn took test results from five countries and found that in

Australia, males scored 0.5 points better than females, while in the other countries (New Zealand, White South Africa, Estonia and Argentina) females scored 0.5 to 1.5 points higher. Flynn attributed these differences to the females being slightly more focused in the testing room, just like they use to be in the classroom – because the tested groups were children aged 14-18. This part generally wasn't reported, probably due to fears people would remember that boys need longer to go through puberty (if I were to employ feminist propaganda methods, I'd phrase it "they need longer to evolve above the basic female form", but let's not go there). The amount of distortion this story experienced is unbelievable. *Cosmopolitan*, for example, starts pretty clever with "According to a study of IQ tests from around the world, women have higher IQs than men"(impressively vague), but then wanders off into the realm of outright fantasy, continuing: "Researcher James Flynn checked out the IQs of people from the U.S., Europe, Canada, New Zealand, Argentine, and Estonia, and found that women came out on top." **(Griffin, 2012)** Obviously, the U.S. and Europe seem to be more impressive than South Africa (especially the "White" South Africa, it sounds so racist), and why Australia is missing is pretty clear.

The story was everywhere. But nobody apart from "Psychology Today" reported Flynn objecting and complaining that his findings have been greatly distorted. **(Kaufman, 2012)** This was just of no interest to the feminist media.

The agenda is clear.

Nobody thinks about boys in school who will get ridiculed for it by equally feminist teachers (some of which even nowadays still perpetuate the myth of the "decaying y-chromosome"). Stuff like this trickles down through newspapers, magazines, TV, social media and the rest of the internet. It would've been a good occasion to include that the male intelligence shows a larger variation; while there is only a slight male advantage in the average IQ (apart from schoolgirls in New Zealand, Argentina, White South Africa and Estonia), the amount of men on the "genius" intelligence level is substantially higher than that of women. **(Hedges & Nowell, 1995)**, **(Deary, Irwing, Der & Bates, 2007)** But in the feminist world, such would be sexist, misogynistic.[3] It has to be noted that none of the media articles, also none of the

---

[3] Theories as to why more men are geniuses include that this phenomenon may be a result of the fact that "all humans are female at the very beginning in the womb, the female is the basic condition" – a point feminists are eager to make, declaring the male a deviation from the norm, and they see it as proof of female superiority. Ignoring, of course, the logical conclusion that the male can as well be interpreted as evolving beyond that basic form, adding information to the genetic basis. In the end, the XX chromosome is containing twice the same information, whereas XY has the X information plus the additional Y. As such it might be easier for men to access their basic incorporated female traits, whereas women never had a state of being male and thus can't access male traits (speaking generally, of course, regarding the whole population)

mentions in feminist blogs and publications, worded it "men and women are now equal in intelligence" (since in one of the countries the boys were ahead and the highest difference was just 1.5 points, and in the past a male advantage of 5 points was considered negligible). It's a pretty one-sided business. But since the feminist narrative is: "You cannot be sexist against men, you cannot discriminate against men", it's okay.

In general, feminism often finds itself at odds with reality and needs to reinterpret it. One of the eternal annoyances is the physical dominance of men, which, logically, is part of any physical interaction between men and women, one of them especially popular: sex. If one wants to see the utterly confused face of feminism, all it takes is a look at this topic. From the feminist fight to get the verb "to fuck" also attributed to women, since it otherwise objectifies women (not only a man fucks a woman, at the same time the woman fucks the man), while at the same time struggling to keep the passive (objectified) role when claiming only the active part (here suddenly only the man again) can rape.

Even the halfway sane feminists that do not claim all heterosexual intercourse is rape do acknowledge that sex is a form of male domination and complain about sex being centered around the male arousal (since the woman needs to be attractive to the man in order to incite an erection and the male orgasm is the natural goal of the whole act). To counter this, they did a lot of pointing out how the female body is superior in regard to sex (a point that even the lesbian core of feminism could rally behind), like how a woman's biggest sexual organ is her skin, how the female orgasm is more intense and longer and overall better, and if a woman has problems to orgasm despite all this superiority, it's clearly the man's fault, because the woman is too objectified or not objectified enough, depending on what theories they follow and how those are interpreted. One thing is for sure, it has got nothing to do with the rather unfortunate placement of the clitoris.

But enough about the feminist struggle with the simple facts that men are stronger and penetration and male orgasm are essential for procreation and how they call it oppression and all this needs to change somehow.

Sex is not the only thing that is sexist and oppressive, science and mathematics are as well. Unforgotten Luce Irigaray's rambling about $E=mc^2$ being "a sexed equation" and how physics prefer solid, rigid objects because they are similar to the male sex organ, and how fluid mechanics (standing for the female sex organ, with menstruation etc.) are oppressed. If we consider this nonsense to be running rampant at our universities for several decades now, ever since feminist "thinking" has invaded education, it comes as no surprise that not many young men feel inclined to pursue higher education or if they do, they prefer to avoid social sciences and humanities.

It's pretty clear that feminism doesn't favor logic, which also has a simple explanation: Many feminists regard logic itself as sexist and oppressive, a method to silence opposition. **(Nye, 1990)** Nye even acknowledges the intent "to take up the words […] and reshape them" and comes to the (logical?) conclusion: "Logic in its final perfection is insane."

Considering such re-definitions of words, it is now clear how feminism could pull its biggest trick, to persuade people that it's an ideology promoting "equal rights". It's essential to understand that, for feminists, "equality" is something fluid, depending on the situation, even meaning inequality. As we've seen with the wage gap myth, "equal pay" can be interpreted in a variety of ways. A woman working twenty hours a week doesn't earn the same as her male colleague that works forty hours a week. It's unequal. Women working as barmaids don't earn the same as male lawyers. It's unequal. Such are the atrocities feminism fights.

Another example are the quotas that are in place or are in process of being implemented in many countries around the world. Companies are obliged to employ at least a certain percentage of women – on all levels. The latest push comes from the EU and calls for a quota of female board directors in European companies. Strategies like this will mean a fast-track to the top for a lot of women, coming at the expense of a lot of men who worked longer, harder and better, just to see the promotion go to the new female colleague. Because women need to be fairly represented everywhere in society. And since women make up fifty percent of the population the goal is fifty percent – or more. It's not equal rights, which would mean equal opportunities; it's equal outcome, with less or no investment. Of course this only goes for the good jobs. It's all about glass ceilings. Not about the glass cellars, jobs women don't want to do, the low-paid, dirty, dangerous work. No true feminist would ask for any kind of "equality" there.

Just as no-one of them asks for a "Domestic Violence Act", only for a "Violence Against Women Act". One of the arguments for lopsided legislature is that women need excess legal power over men to counter men's physical advantage. If a woman is alone with a man, she has to be afraid that he might attack her. To "equalize" this, the man has to be afraid of the woman using her legal powers over him to have him arrested and prosecuted if she only so much as *feels* threatened. If one would adhere to the insanity of logic, it might seem that it's not a valid argument: If the man uses his physical power, it's clearly illegal and she can have him arrested anyway, while her legal powers are, well, legal. Even under nowadays laws, if the man can prove the woman lied, there will usually be no (or just very minor) consequences for her, since women who actually are threatened/abused/raped might otherwise be discouraged to come forward.

With this in mind, an explanation for the eternal self-victimization of feminists offers itself: By inventing an invisible "patriarchy" and putting men in the position of power by simply being men, feminists can demand all kinds of benefits in the name of overall equality. They can forever claim that there's a need for "action", that there's "inequality", because at the very end, men and women aren't equal. They can continue to claim this imbalance needs adjusting through "equal rights", though that doesn't mean what a logical person would assume it means. It's just a play on words, a mind trick insane enough to work, with the help of millions of feminists who ended up in education and media. At least most of them don't follow (openly) the more radical notion that, since men have oppressed women for thousands of years, now it's the women's "right" to equally oppress men for an equally long time to make up for it.

Equality.

It's all a matter of definitions.

Feminism and MRA

This eternal victimization requires one major element: Disadvantages of men can never be acknowledged. "A sorrow shared is a sorrow halved" as the proverb goes, and feminism cannot afford to lose half its impact. So they ignored men's issues, confusing millions of people who believed the big lie of feminists fighting for equal rights – it should've been clear by the word "feminism" alone that this excludes everyone who isn't female. A very weak attempt was made by pointing out that by deconstructing gender roles feminism freed men up to become househusbands and stay-at-home-dads, which already has been an option before; and considering the feminist point of view of housework and raising kids being oppression, such statements can be taken with a grain of salt. But since one of the declared goals of feminism is the destruction of the family, it's pretty moot anyway.

Men had to work longer until retirement than women, even though women have a statistically higher life expectancy. Men were drafted for military service, whereas feminists only fought for women to be able to choose a military career if they want to. Men have no reproductive rights and are routinely ignored in family courts and child custody cases. When on a sinking cruise ship, they were the very last to be allowed on the lifeboats. Women started to earn more than men for the same work, women started to outnumber men at the universities and the increasingly feminist environment made life a living hell for male students and the male population in general.

Men increasingly realized that all the talk about "equality" was just this – talk. They grew tired of hearing about "male privilege", when it clearly were the women who got handed goodies and praise just for having a vagina. Since the turn of the millennium, there is a growing number of *men's rights activists*, who try to address the issues and fight against unjust portrayals of men, for paternal rights and support in education.

Feminists don't take lightly to that. Helping boys to succeed in school? Hell no! Not after their feminist restructuring of classrooms, teacher training and other educational reforms to help girls performing better led to a widening gender gap in higher education. Some even went so far as preparing to celebrate in 2068, when (following a rather absurd calculation) the last man would get his bachelor's degree and after that all higher education would be exclusively female. **(Kohn, 2009)**

Seeing their goal of a female dominated world

endangered by the prospects of boys recovering and maybe even reclaiming their half of seats in education (which would be what feminists hate most, equality), feminists did what they can best: shout and riot. When a professor was scheduled to hold a lecture about how to help boys in school at the university of Toronto, groups of rabid feminists blocked the entry, shouted "no hate-speech on campus", harassed people trying to get into the building and finally attacked police officers who were shielding the entrance. Videos of the event circulate on the internet, and in one particular instance a visitor waiting to get into the building is repeatedly insulted by a feminist. Transcript:

"You're fucking scum. You are fucking scum. You fucking rape apologist, incest supporting, woman hating fucking scum. You're fucking scum." **(Elam, 2012)**

Also, in a surprising demonstration of their verbal variety, they are calling the policemen „fucking pigs".

Ironically, the lecturing professor was a former board member of NOW, the National Organization of Women, and did more for feminism than all of the protestors combined. Well, after some of them attacked the police, were thrown to the ground and handcuffed, they shouted "This is what men's rights look like" and finally switched into familiar territory, playing the victim.

Of course they see any help for men – even for future men: boys -, any attempt to make the male point of view a topic, as a direct attack on feminism. In the best tradition of their insane, murderous mothers they use verbal and physical violence to ensure their goals are not endangered. Any challenge to the feminist narrative will be met with their full force. And since the current culture is dominated by feminism, they have plenty of options. Due to the interpretation "everything that is pro male is anti female", the convenient label "misogynist" was quickly applied to everything concerning the men's rights movement.

Since this movement is pretty much non-existent in the media (why fight something when you can simply ignore it?), nobody really cared. Eventually, since this behavior fails to address the growing concerns, it will only raise the amount of young men who will feel outcast, disenfranchised, discriminated, ridiculed and hated.

Where will this lead us?

The Future

All of this doesn't leave a bright outlook to the future. After all, the increasingly fragile relation between men and women is essential for the survival of the society we live in. In its relentless desire to amend the balance and to shift women in a position of power, feminism had a devastating impact, often even beyond the obvious influences like destruction of the family. With the state taking the role of the father (by providing security, money (in the form of welfare, women-friendly divorce courts and jobs that require nothing more than talking on the phone for a few hours), and care (daycare centers), feminists were jubilant that men were basically unnecessary for raising kids, as society can be perpetuated without them.

Or can't it?

We've seen how feminism aggressively spread the idea of women as sexual selectors in prehistoric times in order to dismiss the following millennia of man-made societies as "oppressive" and even "rape culture" (when it actually have been the prehistoric times that really deserve this title). It's impossible for them to acknowledge these societies made life easier and safer for women. Nonetheless, they generally succeeded in reinterpreting the role of women and nowadays, it's undeniable that feminism made women sexual selectors, too; with stricter laws every year, a man who as much as *approaches* a woman runs the risk of being accused of sexual harassment or at least sexism. So women can choose.

But they don't.

For some reason a lot of women still follow their instinct and wait to be chosen. But men, now having to fear for their jobs or even freedom, hesitate. Nobody wants to find himself caught in the increasingly narrow definitions of rape. The best thing is to just sit back and let the woman do everything, to be as safe as possible.

But some women don't even want to choose, because they can't be satisfied anymore. Feminism thoroughly destroyed the image of masculinity, ridiculed it and depicted men as either losers or oppressors. The social status of men has been changed to "undesirable". So any properly indoctrinated woman wouldn't want a man, apart from the very desperate ones that later in life just try to get impregnated and then swiftly get rid of the man (she'll accept his money, though, and even sue for it).

Now, men aren't that stupid. They see the growing number of divorces initiated by women (the majority of divorces; among college-educated couples up to 90%), they see that they usually get the short stick in divorce court (according to a 2004 survey, women end up getting a better settlement than men in 60% of cases, men only in 10%), and they are aware that there's yet another unacceptable risk: Kids for which they pay but rarely see.

Also, the woman is not perceived as partner anymore. Back in the old days, a man fought at work and came home to his wife and family. Women were a symbol of relaxation (apart from the nagging, of course), a personified sanctuary from the turbulences of the outside world. Feminism changed it, and it changed it dramatically. The price for being viewed as equal was losing this special status. A woman became another competitor in the outside world. Even worse, feminism added the battle of the sexes and made women an enemy. Constant media barrage about women being superior didn't exactly help to avoid men getting disappointed in the way they are disrespected. An increasing number of young men now aren't even interested in dating anymore and prefer living a life of fun and games – without women.

Of course the occasional sex takes place. Thanks to AIDS - and men's awareness of possible entrapment with a child - it is usually safe. Sometimes part of these considerations are unnecessary, as the participating woman may be interested in intercourse, but not in children. Ironically, feminism claimed women can do everything men do, and do it better, while taking away the only thing women actually do better: being a mother. Women feel the social pressure to work due to the outlawed, "obsolete and oppressive" role as mother and housewife. They are expected to take a day off, give birth, and go back to work the next day. Not only is it important in order not to drag down the women's wage statistics, but also because it's the only way she can be liberated and empowered. In order to do so, the mother wakes her kid in the morning, drops it off at the daycare and picks it up again in the evening, to put it to sleep at home. Repeat. Repeat. Repeat. They have similar concerns as the men who are afraid of getting handed a divorce: To have kids which they will rarely see and have any connection with.

Even if, for some unknown reason, an insane woman manages to find an equally insane male cohabitant and successfully "selects" him, chances are that she falls victim to one of her reproductive rights: the pill. Research shows that the contraceptive pill can hinder a woman's natural ability to detect a man genetically dissimilar to herself, which may "result in difficulties when trying to conceive, an increased risk of miscarriage and long intervals between pregnancies." **(Roberts, Gosling, Carter & Petrie, 2008)**

All of this liberating and empowering mess

results in the demise of the society which created it. A self-destruction of the white western nations, whose civilization brought unprecedented wealth and security and thus nourished the cancer that is now devouring it. Birth rates are tumbling down for those infected with this ideology, and the affected nations desperately try to fill the gaps with immigrants from other cultures who do not suffer from feminism and are constantly growing. Will this be the antidote? Will this injection of fresh blood stop the deadly disease? Feminism aimed to destroy men (even the less radical fight the "rape culture", "the patriarchy"), and in its attempts, it destroys western culture as a whole.

Who will scavenge the ruins?

Will Islam prevail, and women will lose their right to dress like sluts (hey, feminists invented and named "slut walks"), a right for which many men fought and died?

Or will it be the Chinese, ever growing and wise enough to deliver an occasional reality check to their women - a piece from the state organization for women's rights read: "The tragedy is, they don't realize that as women age, they are worth less and less." **(Magistad, 2013)** Sure to cause a wave of uproar in the media, seemingly hypocritical after calling men for decades "obsolete", "unnecessary" and "a disease". But as we know, equal treatment never was on the feminist agenda, so such outrage makes perfect sense. Also, the Chinese interpretation makes sense: As we've seen, women are extremely valuable for society, as they are needed to reproduce, and this ability is even more precious due to the limited potential (usually only one or two children per women, almost a year until next pregnancy, they need long care after birth). Women are valuable for society – but only as long as they fulfill this duty. Feminism "liberates" an increasing number from this duty, it encourages women to forfeit the role of the mother and choose a business career instead. Reproductive rights, contraception and abortion helped as well in making women less worth for society. Women got freed from their responsibility, it was made an option, and feminists did all they could to discourage women from choosing this option. We remember Simone de Beauvoir who said: "Women should not have that choice". The existence of our society became the sole responsibility and the free choice of women – and they failed. Our society declines, our future vanishes.

Recognizing this, who would hold their attitude against those other nations? They've seen the devastating impact of feminism and don't want to go down that road to hell with us. When a policewoman slapped a man in Tunisia in 2010, it was not only a deadly insult, it was also a preview of things to come, should the

Western oriented governments not be taken down. Not having been subject to the slow mutation of women's rights into feminist control of society, they felt the pain that the west has gradually grown used to in a more immediate manner and fought back. The Arab Spring was born. Traditional Islamists regained heavy influence. The immolation of one man sparked a firestorm, and it is yet to determine how badly it burned the cause for women's rights in those countries. A cause that is just, by the way – it doesn't hurt to say it again. There's nothing wrong with equal opportunities (*equal* as a sane person would understand it); not when it's paired with mutual respect and responsibilities. But unfortunately, such a women's rights movement doesn't exist. There's only feminism, and it's a hideous burlesque which has dropped its mask long ago.

Will the West wake up and see? The men surely are realizing that they've been told lies, and are increasingly aware how they are portrayed in the media. The rise of men's rights activists gives evidence of this slow awakening. When feminists get too brazen, like in Sweden, they sometimes get called out, like when they tried to impose a "man tax". **(Chamberlain, 2005)** Unfortunately, they keep on trying. Long ago some women fought for equal opportunities and got them, then feminists fought for equal outcome with less investment (earning the same while working less), and when they couldn't manipulate the statistics anymore and it became clear women have gained massive advantages, this inequality was celebrated. Anyone who criticizes this hypocrisy gets labeled a misogynist, sexist or an oppressive tool of the patriarchy. They want to stay the victims to demand more and more compensation and power.

What is the endgame, e.g. in the topic of rape? It's easy to envision feminists argue that – since sexual activities lead to arousal in the woman, which leads to the release of endorphins that act like drugs – a woman loses her ability to legally consent as soon as foreplay begins, thus any consensual intercourse is rape. Or maybe it will be the ubiquitous oppression through the patriarchy, which puts women under constant pressure and is forcing all of her behavior, including giving consent.

Whatever it will be, one thing is for sure: Men will be at fault.

And nobody needs to be more aware of that than men themselves. So, in order to get this message into the heads of boys (so they won't speak up later in life), feminism needs to be taught in schools, even more than before. In a message on Twitter, the National Women's Studies Association confirmed that one of the topics of their 2013 conference will be "Teaching Boys Feminism". Because that's fair. The same rabid feminists that fight tooth and nails against anyone who tries to support boys in schools are going to teach those boys feminism. How it's okay that girls get advantages that are denied to boys. How boys and men are oppressors, beneficiaries of the patriarchy; how women are eternal victims, and when they earn more, it's "not sexist, but fair". **(Hinsliff, 2011)**[4]

We should probably be thankful if they choose more appropriate words than that used by the feminist mentioned earlier, when she protested against a lecture about how to help boys who struggle in school. Let's hear them once again:

"You're fucking scum. You are fucking scum. You fucking rape apologist, incest supporting, woman hating fucking scum. You're fucking scum."

Will this be the message feminists want to teach boys? The NWSA's Twitter message didn't provide such details, but at least it didn't include the latest (May 2013) trending feminist hashtag:

#killallmen

And just like with Solana's SCUM (this word

---

[4] In the same article, Hinsliff tries to spin this as a good thing for men, as it allegedly shows that feminism did not cut into men's wages, it just raised women to and beyond the same level. This ignores the stagnant wages since introduction of feminism as mentioned earlier. **(Sorscher, 2011)** Considering this, men indeed lost up to half their wages over time.

seems to have an unholy appeal with feminists), more moderate feminists – who are just out for control, or at least don't want their murderous ambitions out in the open (yet?) – are quick to play it down with notions of the patriarchy, which wields all the power, so it's not a real threat, just a fantasy, which is totally understandable regarding the oppression of women etc.

Okay.

Now, why not make it equal? Why not teach girls about society's perception of the "disposability of males"? Why not teach girls to respect men and honor them for creating a world that gives even the weakest a fair chance? Feminism only knows one direction of respect, and it certainly is not towards men. Time and time again they prove beyond a doubt that there is nothing equal, nothing mutual on their agenda. Just like money, just like power, respect is something that has to go from men to women – exclusively.

This is especially cruel as boys are actually growing up in a matriarchy, and this is not some paranoid conspiracy theory. From the earliest age, it's mothers – increasingly single mothers - who influence their children, it's daycare workers and elementary school teachers, all overwhelmingly female. There's a substantial and growing lack of male role models, and additionally the feminist propaganda in the media, as fake and manipulated as it is, trickles down through the ever-present channels of the information age, unfiltered, unrectified, unopposed. Instead, it is often embraced by feminist indoctrinated personnel, as they are fighting oppression. And as we see, even this is still not enough indoctrination for feminists.

The very last thing boys need, is more of the same. But that's the essence of feminism – never stop, always push it one step further, with no regard to reason, peace or truth.

How to stop the madness? Just doing the same feminism did, shoveling people of the other gender into those positions, will not work, as any man trying to get into media and education has to follow the established narrative, and since anything encouraging men is considered misogyny, it won't be allowed. The best hope for the survival of our society rests, as it seems, on the common sense of the general population – an adventurous prospect. But more and more people are waking up to the lies and distortions of modern feminism, particularly due to its above mentioned need to go further, to constantly grow, like cancer, until nobody can ignore the ugly excrescence any longer, no matter how much make-up feminists apply to conceal its true destructive nature. Will the inevitable chemotherapy come timely enough to purge that evil from our midst? Will that ugly siren that wails on and on finally be silenced?

The answer to that question lies out there, ahead, in the unchartered waters of the future. All we can do is what we have done since the dawn of mankind: To boldly steer into this fog, to hope for the best and expect the worst.

Bibliography

Ackerman, Elise (2013, February 24).
Superiority of Female Workers Confirmed:
Study Finds Women Really Do Work Longer And
Harder Than Men. *Forbes* , p. online.
http://www.forbes.com/sites/eliseackerman/2
013/02/24/superiority-of-female-workers-
confirmed-study-finds-women-really-do-work-
longer-and-harder-than-men/

Alfonsi, Sharyn. (2010, September 1).
Reverse Gender Gap: Study Says Young,
Childless Women Earn More Than Men. *ABC
World News* , p. online.
http://abcnews.go.com/WN/reverse-gender-
gap-study-young-childless-women-
earn/story?id=11538401#.UecExMo9WAE

Al Jazeera (2013, March 7). #tooFEW
feminists engage Wikipedia. *Al Jazeera: The
Stream*, p. online
http://stream.aljazeera.com/story/201303072
321-0022594

Blech, Jörg; von Bredow, Rafaela (2003,
September 15). Eine Krankheit namens Mann.
Der Spiegel , p. online.
http://www.spiegel.de/spiegel/print/d-
28591080.html

Chamberlain, Andrew (2005). *Externalities
and the Swedish Man Tax.* Tax Foundation, p.
online
http://taxfoundation.org/blog/externalities
-and-swedish-man-tax

Clay, Gibbons & Hood (2007). *Dubay v. Wells.* Michigan: United States Court of Appeals.
http://www.ca6.uscourts.gov/opinions.pdf/07 a0442p-06.pdf

de Beauvoir, Simone (1975, June 14). Interview with Simone de Beauvoir: Sex, Society, and the Female Dilemma. *Saturday Review* , p. 18.

Deary, Ian J.; Irwing, Paul; Der, Geoff & Bates, Timothy C. (2007, September-October n/a). Brother-sister differences in the g factor in intelligence: Analysis of full, opposite-sex siblings from the NLSY1979. *Intelligence* , pp. 451-456.
http://www.sciencedirect.com/science/articl e/pii/S0160289606001115

Elam, Paul (2012). *http://www.avoiceformen.com/feminism/vanja-krajina-university-of-toronto/.* Toronto: n/a.
http://www.avoiceformen.com/feminism/vanja-krajina-university-of-toronto/
Video:
http://www.youtube.com/watch?v=iARHCxAMAO0

FAZ/dapd. (2012, Dezember 15). In Deutschland verdienen Frauen deutlich weniger. *FAZ* , p. online.
http://www.faz.net/frankfurter-allgemeine-zeitung/beruf-und-chance/einkommen-in-deutschland-verdienen-frauen-deutlich-weniger-11993503.html

Griffin, Christie (2012, n/a n/a). 14 Things Women Do Better Than Men. *Cosmopolitan* , p. online.
http://www.cosmopolitan.com/advice/tips/women-better-than-men-things#slide-2

Hedges, L.V., & Nowell, A. (1995, July 7). Sex differences in mental test scores, variability, and numbers of high-scoring individuals. *Science* , pp. 41-45.
http://www.ncbi.nlm.nih.gov/pubmed/7604277

Heflin, Krista. J. (2012, September 10). Gender-based Abortion - Abort the Males . *Fethez Hub (Blog) Femitheism - Femitheist* , p. online.
http://femitheistreborn.blogspot.de/2012/09/gender-based-abortion-abort-males.html

Herzog, Hal (2012, August 22). Why Are Rape Victims More - Not Less - Likely to Become Pregnant? *Psychology Today*, p. online.
http://www.psychologytoday.com/blog/animals-and-us/201208/why-are-rape-victims-more-not-less-likely-become-pregnant

Hinsliff, Gaby (2011). Young women are now earning more than men - that's not sexist, just fair. *The Observer* , p. online.
http://www.guardian.co.uk/commentisfree/2011/nov/27/young-women-earning-more-men

Hughes, Sarah Anne (2011). 'The Talk' ladies under fire for laughing at Catherine Kieu story. *Washington Post* , p. online.
http://www.washingtonpost.com/blogs/celebritology/post/the-talk-ladies-under-fire-for-laughing-at-catherine-kieu-story-video/2011/07/18/gIQA3OjkLI_blog.html
Video:
http://www.youtube.com/watch?v=nrvDhSB7GHk

Kaufman, Scott Barry (2012). Men, Women, and IQ: Setting the Record Straight. *Psychology Today* , p. online. http://www.psychologytoday.com/blog/beautiful-minds/201207/men-women-and-iq-setting-the-record-straight

Knapp, Fred (2008, November 21). Neb. Lawmakers Put Age Limit On Safe Haven Law. *npr* , p. online. http://www.npr.org/templates/story/story.php?storyId=97317532

Kohn, David (2009, February 11). The Gender Gap: Boys Lagging. *CBS News* , p. online. http://www.cbsnews.com/8301-18560_162-527678.html

Magistad, Mary Kay (2013). China's 'leftover women', unmarried at 27 . *BBC News Magazine* , p. online. http://www.bbc.co.uk/news/magazine-21320560

McKie, Robin (2002). Men redundant? Now we don't need women either. *The Guardian* , p. online. http://www.guardian.co.uk/world/2002/feb/10/medicalscience.research

NBC/AP. (2010, January 13). Men more evolved? Their Y chromosome is. *NBC News* , p. online. http://www.nbcnews.com/id/34843925/ns/health-mens_health/t/men-more-evolved-their-y-chromosome/

Nye, Andrea (1990). *Words of Power: A Feminist Reading of the History of Logic.* New York, London: Routledge.

Roberts, Dr. Craig; Gosling, Prof. Morris; Carter, Vaughan; Petrie, Prof. Marion (2008). *Contraceptive pill influences partner choice.* Liverpool: University of Liverpool.
http://news.liv.ac.uk/2008/08/13/contraceptive-pill-influences-partner-choice/

Rosin, Hanna (2010, June 8). The End of Men. *The Atlantic* , p. online.
http://www.theatlantic.com/magazine/archive/2010/07/the-end-of-men/308135/

RP (2012). Männer ähneln Affen mehr als Frauen. *Rheinische Post* , p. online.
http://www.rp-online.de/wissen/forschung/maenner-aehneln-affen-mehr-als-frauen-1.2883383

Sommers, Christina Hoff (2012, November 04). Wage Gap Myth Exposed - By Feminists. *Huffington Post* , p. online.
http://www.huffingtonpost.com/christina-hoff-sommers/wage-gap_b_2073804.html

Sorscher, Stan (2011, January 28). Making Business Succeed. *Huffington Post,* p. online
http://www.huffingtonpost.com/stan-sorscher/making-business-succeed_b_812684.html

United States Children's Bureau. (2012). *"Child Maltreatment 2011".* Washington, D.C.: US Department of Health and Human Services, p. 59
http://www.acf.hhs.gov/sites/default/files/cb/cm11.pdf

Voss, Julia (2013). Steinzeit für immer. *FAZ* , p. online. **http://www.faz.net/aktuell/feuilleton/debat ten/anti-emanzipatorische-argumente-steinzeit-fuer-immer-12125657.html**

Wood, Wendy, & Eagly, Alice H. (2002, Vol. 128 No. 5). A Cross-Cultural Analysis of the Behaviour of Women and Men: Implications for the Origin of Sex Differences. *Psychological Bulletin, American Psychological Association, Inc.* , pp. 699-727.